Alisa E Clark **Mindfulness Paintings**

A Book of Creative Meditation Exercises, Artwork & Art Activities

Acknowledgements:

Editing and Creative Support by Emily Clark

Peacock and Buttons 2, 2016

Permissions:

Bulk orders can be purchased through www.MindfulnessPaintings.com
Mindfulness Paintings is also available from Amazon.com and other book stores.

Instructions:

Look for the pages within this book titled "Something to Try." When reading them, begin at the center of the spiral. From there, follow any arrows or stars; they will lead you through the activity. Enjoy your mindfulness journey!

Peacock and Buttons 3, 2016

Note to the Reader:

You will find some of my creative journaling inside this book. My journaling process is similar to my art making process. With this comes a little bit of unsophistication. I may fail to explain every thought fully. Things are a little disorganized. I look on these entries as creative expression, so I allow myself the liberty to be spontaneous. A little blunder here and there gets bypassed so I can preserve this spontaneity. I'm sharing my art process, not my product, with these hand written entries. I challenge you to embrace the imperfections as well so your process is not compromised. See me meeting this challenge and note that I am fearlessly flawed. Join me in that spirit as we journey through this book and create mindfulness paintings together.

Embrace the imperfections.
Join me in being fearlessly flawed.

Dear Reader,

I consciously disregarded traditional form as I created this book. Any oddities, misspellings, blemishes or digressions that transpired as I worked have not been edited out. Please forgive the peculiar composition and numerous imperfections. Conventions would have distracted me from my goal: embracing a process that allows me to be more mindful, more cognizant, and more fully present. Maybe my process will help you notice something? Maybe "Something to Try" will make you more aware? It would be splendiferous if we, together, could explore and find new ways to be more fully MINDFUL.

With you, Alisa

Something to Try

gritty   smooth   hard   rough   slippery   bumpy   flat   soft

Pick a tool: a pen, a paint brush, a crayon??? Move it across a surface. Get lost in what is happening right now. Focus on the feel of your tool in your hand. Notice how your tool feels on your surface. Consider it a quiet voice that doesn't have any real power. Notice it. If you notice the pressure of what others might think, don't push it away. But, perhaps, don't indulge it.

spongy   squishy   gravelly   flexible   stiff   rugged   uneven

Crazy Colors, 2018

Something to Think About:

When I made this painting, I couldn't stop myself from making flowers that were painted crazy colors. I had to drift away from the voice that was telling me to paint the red flowers a red color. I let myself be free from the constraint of "making them look real." I realized that the "real stuff" is what the world calls "art." Today, I ponder how I have stacks of paintings others may consider garbage. To me, they're all treasures. Consider how painting can give you a place where you get to make all the decisions and break all the rules. Ponder how your mind and body can wander as you use colors and shapes in the way that pleases you in the moment. As you let colors pop, you might notice that you feel satisfaction. As you mix your paints, you can enjoy the ways the colors swirl and change. Do you believe YOU CAN DO WHATEVER YOU WANT on your canvas? Be mindful of how you feel about your creation. Notice that you are free from the judgements of others here. Every choice you make is yours. It's all about the process, not the product. Free yourself from anyone's expectations, including yours.

It's all about the process, not the product.
Free yourself from anyone's expectations, including yours.

Mindfulness ~~Expert~~

I am no expert in mindfulness nor am I ordinarily good at being present in the moment. Art making, however, allows me a place where I can be more present. With each stroke of my brush, I am more "in the moment," experiencing more freedom, and _gently_ noticing things: things that would normally cause me considerable anxiety, stress, and fear. As I paint, I hear the hum of the words "~~the process~~ NOT the product": my college art education's department's _mantra_ that has wormed its way into all the nerve cells of my "creative brain." This hum has guided me to "just create" with a child-like freedom and an openness

I had no idea how much this has influenced me.

to go wherever my thoughts take me. Art making - somehow mystically - allows me to experience moments of full presentness. I don't know how this happens. I only know that it does happen. I want to unwrap my art making process for you. I will do my best to let you hear what I hear as I move my brush across a canvas. I will try to share what I notice and experience as I do something simple like choose a color, a shape, or a texture. You may hear what I hear or notice what I notice. Or, you may find that you hear or notice something radically different as you create. Don't worry about your level of expertise. Don't let your perception of your "talent" stop you from making

Embrace the Process

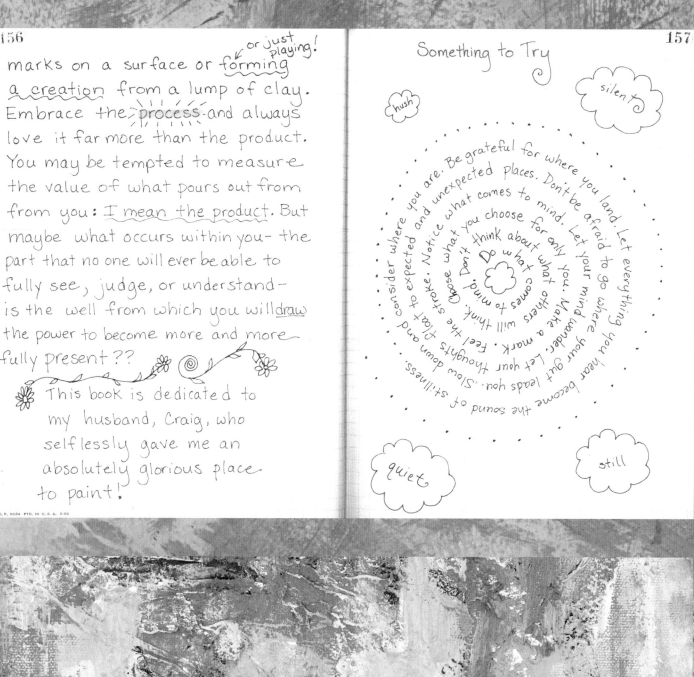

or just playing!

marks on a surface or forming
a creation from a lump of clay.
Embrace the process and always
love it far more than the product.
You may be tempted to measure
the value of what pours out from
from you: I mean the product. But
maybe what occurs within you— the
part that no one will ever be able to
fully see, judge, or understand—
is the well from which you will draw
the power to become more and more
fully present ??

This book is dedicated to
my husband, Craig, who
selflessly gave me an
absolutely glorious place
to paint!

Something to Try

hush

silent

consider where you are. Be grateful for where you land. Let everything you hear become the sound of stillness. Slow down and let your thoughts float. Don't be afraid to go where your mind leads you. Make a mark. Feel the stroke. Notice what you choose for only you. Let what comes to mind. Don't think about what others will think. Choose what comes to mind. Do what

quiet

still

Be Fully Present

Eyeball Flowers, 2018

Something to Think About:

As I made this painting, I was happy, even though the product looks like it was made by a child. I don't have earth shattering artistic ability. Painting isn't supposed to be about achieving greatness. What made me most happy as I painted was the experience. I wasn't worried about what the world would think. I felt content as the color flowed across the surface. I felt calm, which is a big deal since I am a person who ordinarily has a constant motor running inside. Focusing on the process let me slow down and notice what was happening right in front of me. I didn't get dragged down by the millions of thoughts that usually race inside my head. You can harness this same stillness. Consider the power painting can give you: the power to be in the moment. Ponder how that power gives you the unique opportunity to slow down and calm down. Meditate on how you feel as you paint. Be sucked into the quietness. Watch your paint brush and enjoy the colors. Be mindful of your mood and celebrate peace.

Be drawn into the quietness. Be mindful of your mood and celebrate peace.

Aware

10/4/2018

Today I will be aware of my past. ;;
I will make something new from
the old. I will capture things and
keep them on my canvas.

Layers and layers of <u>color</u> make the the object. My paintbrush feels. I am aware of my surface vibrate. There are so many thoughts, but I'm more aware of all the colors. My thoughts bounce around.

Is an accidental brushstroke a mistake or an opportunity?

← mistake?

Colors. The colors. Textures. I feel the brush strokes. It's like my paintbrush touches mind wander. My mind free to let my

things I fear, but they are distant when I paint. I escape.

Something to Think About:

Aware doesn't mean you don't notice what came before the moment you are presently in. Painting lets you gently notice what comes to mind. You can let the old stuff drift in and out of consciousness. As you choose a color and enjoy the pleasure of watching the color flow on the canvas, you can be aware of both past and present. As thoughts mingle, you can feel the contour of your subject and be mindful of everything that comes and goes in your mind. Painting time can give your past new power as you realize something new about something old. The process frees you to be present even as you escape to the quietest of places.

Realize something new....

Something to Try: Escape!

Get lost. Be aware of what's happening now.

Let your Paint brush be aware of the contour of the objects, it explores.

You don't have to be in the past.
You can be in this moment.
You can capture the present.

your Paint brush feel the bumps, dips and bounbles...

Feel with your brush. Notice now. Be in the now.

Let your mind wander and let it wonder. Be aware and, at the same time, let your thoughts go.

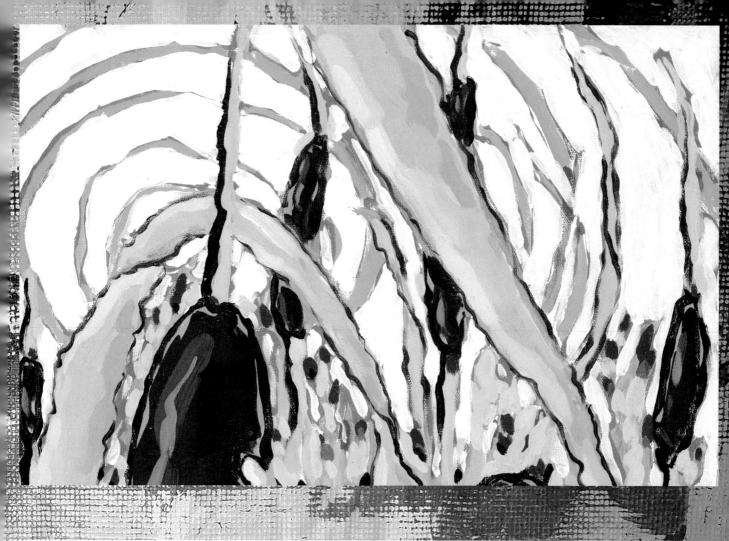

Noticing
10/3/2018

Today I notice that I'm hungry, but it's not time to eat. The pit of my stomach feels hollow. I feel light headed. I've had a snack and it's not helping. Why do I suddenly want to eat now that I have a chance to paint? I try not to push the feeling away. It rises up strong. Ughh. I feel like crap today. My painting is ironic. My cattails look like pickles. I see food everywhere. I'm going to let myself feel it as I paint and see what happens. Maybe I'll forget it all....

mixed with purple ↓   white →

color takes over...

Everything melts away. I get lost. I forget it all.

Make the cucumbers purple? ✓
Milkweed light blue? ✓
It's time to eat and I've forgotten that I'm hungry. I'm lost in 3 paintings at the same time; My worries and thoughts hum in the background. I notice that they are there, but they don't take over. I see them, but I don't really speak to them. The things that usually consume me just hang out like a familiar friend.

I refuse to judge the product. I embrace the process.

The things that usually consume me just hang out like a familiar friend.

I paint and find myself inside a private and wonderful world.

Purple Pickle Painting, 2018

Something to Think About:

My Purple Pickle Painting shows me that there is a transition between my regular state of mind and my state of mind when I am painting. When I first pick up the brush, I am distracted. Painting is a meditation exercise. I have to trust the process that eventually allows me to enter a state of peacefulness. I'm not always in the mood when I first pick up my brush. Just a few minutes into it, I forget what is going on around me. Everything melts away, and I am in my own secret world. If you are like me, you will have to remember that there is space between when you pick up your paint brush and when you experience the pleasure of being in the present moment. You won't slip away with the first stroke, but with a little time you will likely find yourself in a whole new world.

Something to Think About:

My meanderings might seem mindless, but I was mindful of my choices. On the next page, you will see a painting that only a few people I know will understand. If you are from my family of origin, my mindless meanderings will hold great meaning for you. The checks I incorporated into the painting will make my sister want to both laugh and cry. Someone looking in from the outside might wonder why I ruined the whole thing with what looks like a bunch of strange choices. All I know is that the experience let me feel alive. I felt joy. I felt sorrow. I felt love. I even felt God right there with me as I made each and every choice. Consider not letting the voices of others get inside your head as you paint. Don't let those voices rob you of the chance to be drawn into a world of color that brings the incredible opportunity to be fully present. Hear only what comes from within you.

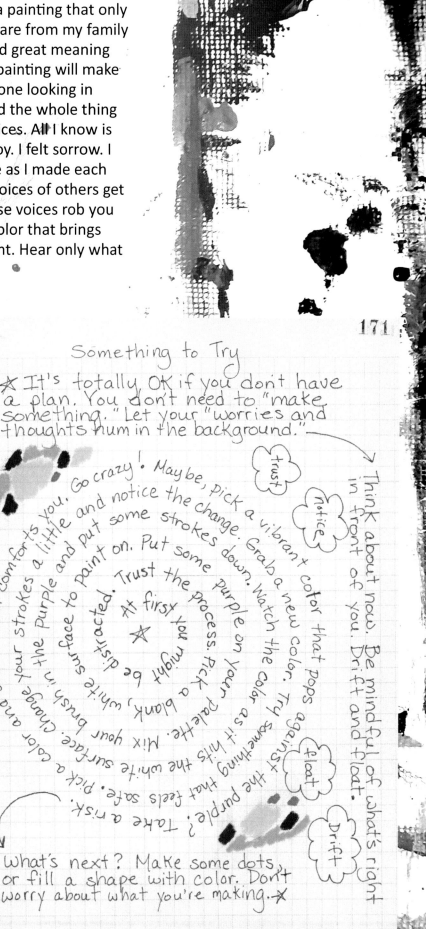

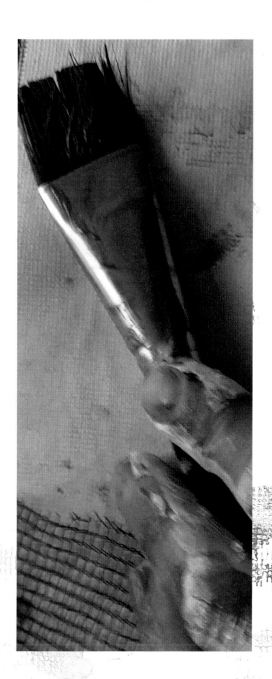

Something to Try

★ It's totally OK if you don't have a plan. You don't need to "make something." Let your "worries and thoughts hum in the background."

Think about now. Be mindful of what's right in front of you. Drift and float.

trust
notice
float
Drift

Go crazy! Maybe, pick a vibrant color that pops against the purple? Take a risk. Pick a color and stroke that comforts you. Go crazy! Maybe, pick a vibrant color that pops against the purple and notice the change. Grab a new color. Watch the color as it hits the white surface. Pick a blank, white surface to paint on. Put some purple and put some strokes down. Mix your brush in the purple and change your strokes a little and notice the change. Trust the process. At first you might be distracted. Change a color and stroke that comforts you.

What's next? Make some dots, or fill a shape with color. Don't worry about what you're making. ★

Mindless Meanderings 10/7/2018

I wasn't sure I could make the old checks work with the rest of the collage. It's a good problem to work through because it's mindless. I just play around with the textures and colors until the solution unfolds. The solution is whatever satisfies me:

me. Today my art has taken me on a quiet journey. I feel.

What I'm mindful of surprises

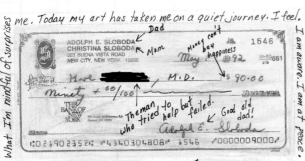

Dad
Mom
Money can't buy happiness
ADOLPH E. SLOBODA
CHRISTINA SLOBODA
323 BUENA VISTA ROAD
NEW CITY, NEW YORK 10956
1546
May @ 92
$90.00
Ninety + 00/100
M.D.
The man who tried to help but failed.
Good old dad!
Adolph E. Sloboda

I am aware. I am at peace.

Add color →
looks like quilt pieces

Buttons, yarn, fabric, tissue paper, more buttons, a key: I can use what I want.

My dad kept all his old checks. When he died, my sister gave me them for my artwork. I've collected some stuff my dad kept in his desk. More than just checks. His scientific research, notes and cards he appreciated, random receipts: all delicious material for my collages. The checks are my favorite because they remind me of things we did, important places we went and the values of my mother and father. The yellow check reminds me of my dad's devotion to my mom. All those trips to Dr. ████. Dad never gave up on mom. These things are the mindless meanderings of art making.

I didn't even know this is where I was going, but here I am.

My mindless, but mindful, meanderings of art making.
Join me in getting lost in the possiblities.

Old Checks, 2018

Something to Try

Do something totally unexpected. Add something to your painting:

- a meaningful object

or

- create a new texture (scrape the surface of your paint with a fork, for example)

Go somewhere you didn't intend to go. Only you and your choices matter right now. Get lost in the possibilities.

← Example: These numbers are meaningful to me. It's where I ended up going. It's OK if you don't understand.

Noticing Distractions

Distractions. ~~When I paint the distractions have a quieter voice.~~ They're not in charge. It's like I've sent them to the basement and shut the door. I pick the next color I'm going to use and all the distractions melt away. I breathe in deeply and let the air out. My muscles relax. I could stay here forever. The product matters, but not in the way you might think it would. There is something incredibly satisfying about feeling satisfied. I like the product: that's what matters. I know what it means. It says what I wanted it to say. The colors and textures communicate what

I set out for them to communicate. Today, I ^suddenly don't see my distraction melt away so easily. A ^giant category 5 hurricane just hit the Pan Handle in Florida. Mexico City is gone. What color do I paint for that? Do I not "notice" the feelings and just keep painting? ↙ps: the news will give anyone feelings Maybe today is a day to let the "distractions" be right in the forefront of my thoughts. ↙"notice" that my thoughts are loud today Sadly, my thoughts don't do me, or anyone else, any good. Sometimes I think I need to let the distractions lead me to act. Take a step, Alisa. Then you might notice that your ~~distractions are just the truth trying to be heard.~~

What matters more: what you notice or what you do about what you notice???

I've sent them to the basement and shut the door. I pick the next color I'm going to use and all the distractions melt away. I breathe in deeply and let the air out. My muscles relax. I could stay here forever. The product matters, but not in the way you might think it would. There

hit the Pan Handle in Florida, Mexico City is gone. What color do I paint for that? Do I not "notice" the feelings and just keep painting? Maybe today is a day to let the "distractions" be right in the forefront of my thoughts. Sadly, my thoughts don't

ps: the news will give anyone feelings

"notice" that my thoughts are loud today

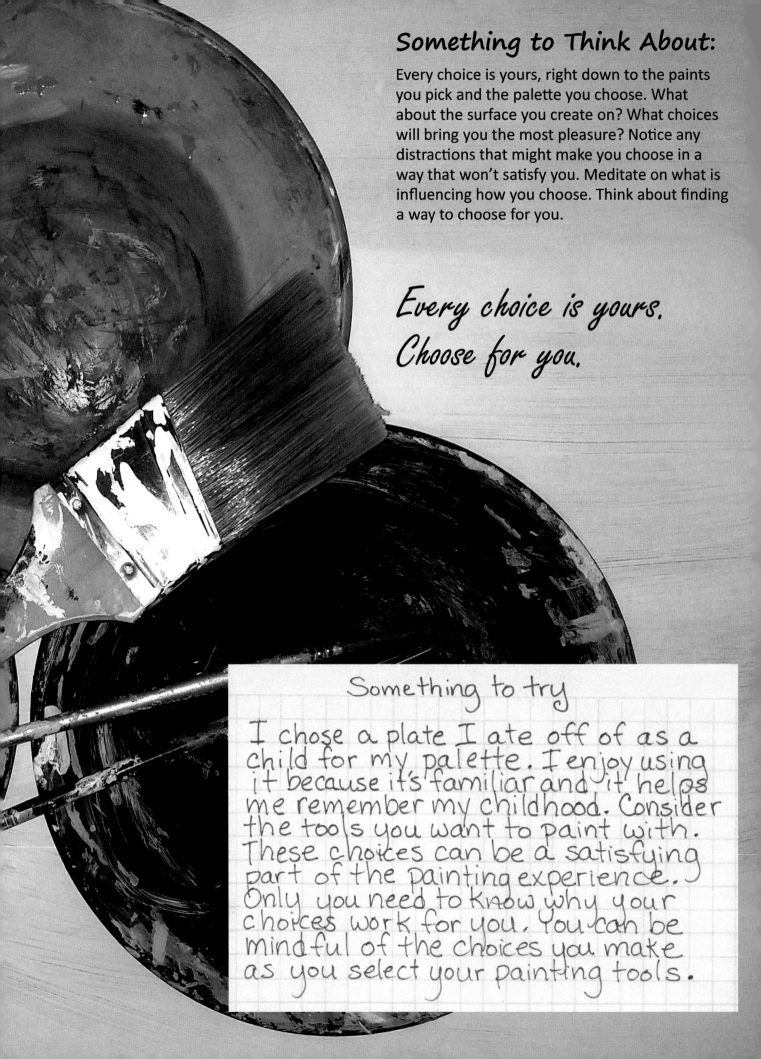

Something to Think About:

Every choice is yours, right down to the paints you pick and the palette you choose. What about the surface you create on? What choices will bring you the most pleasure? Notice any distractions that might make you choose in a way that won't satisfy you. Meditate on what is influencing how you choose. Think about finding a way to choose for you.

Every choice is yours.
Choose for you.

Something to try

I chose a plate I ate off of as a child for my palette. I enjoy using it because it's familiar and it helps me remember my childhood. Consider the tools you want to paint with. These choices can be a satisfying part of the painting experience. Only you need to know why your choices work for you. You can be mindful of the choices you make as you select your painting tools.

Breath Drawing

Breathing exercises make my head hurt. I think about my breath and suddenly it feels like I can't take enough air in. I feel tired and depressed. I'm trying to paint my breath today. I just think about my breath and notice what it's like. I don't try and change my breathing patterns.

I notice 4 types of breath:

Breath # 1: Normal

*I'm going to make this painting part of something bigger. *

I like how it always ends up looking like a child made it. (My art, that is)

Not too deep.

Not too short.

Relaxed & happy.

*Rip it up and make it new.

*I am free to do what occurs to me in the moment.

Breath # 2: Excited

Full of energy. Deeper. Faster.

Breath # 3: Anxious

Maybe "anxious" isn't negative: it's just part of who I am.

Don't push these feelings away. See them as a positive.

Tense. Shallow. Fast.

Breath # 4: Relaxed

*Reinvent it.

A tid bit deeper. Slower. Like waves.

Breath in. Breath out. Breath in. Breath out. Breath in. Breath out. Every breath is from God. It's all good.

Something to Try:

Pick a light color for a base layer. It can have a lot of intensity (brightness) or just a little. Cover your painting surface with this color. Now, choose another color. When you choose it, consider how it will act against your base layer. Will the new color pop or hide? Will the color combination be unsettling or peaceful? Add dots or small strokes of this second color to your canvas. Now, pick a third color. Ponder how the new color will change the surface and mood or your painting. Place this new color down while using a variety of strokes: short, long, thin, straight, wide, squiggly, curvy, etc. Notice how the colors and shapes dance together. Take a moment to meditate on what you see. Stop and think about your thinking. In what ways did you become more mindful as you played with colors and shapes through this simple exercise? You can expand this activity by adding more layers of color. Additional layers of paint add depth and cause the colors to vibrate, dance, and move on your canvas. Try researching "abstract pointillism" to get a feel for how you might vary this exercise. Don't compare yourself to these other artists. Search only for ideas that can help you have a more mindful painting experience. The possibilities are endless and none of them are right or wrong. They are simply choices you can use to enter the "Mindful Zone" and discover something new for your painter's toolbox.

The possibilites are endless, and none of them are right or wrong. Discover something new for your painter's toolbox!

Something to try

your own body's responses. Breathing is just one way your body responds to experiences and painting is just one way to capture how your body's feeling and responding.

Breath in! Be mindful of how you feel about your breathing. Try not to judge it. There are no rules here. Your breath is what it is. Use painting as a way to explore how well you understand your own body's responses.

Be mindful of how your breath feels. Your color might match your breath. Orange for anxious? Yellow for excited? Blue for calm? Try using paint to show how your breath feels. Does it change? Try a long stroke for a deep breath, or a short stroke for a quick or shallow breath. Consider what color might match your breath. Does it feel cool as you paint. Notice how you take it in? Is it shallow or deep? Try a long stroke across a surface. Begin to move some paint across a surface.

Think about your breath as you paint.

Breathe in. Breath out!

Breathe in.
Breathe out.
Breathe in
Breathe out.
Breathe in.
Breathe out.
Breathe in
Breathe out.

Create

Mind Wandering

When I'm creating, my mind naturally wanders. My thoughts float around. I make choices that don't have any real consequence, but they mean something to me. I make choices about textures, choices about colors and choices about shapes. To others it all looks pretty meaningless, but to me it all means something. I'm communicating with my choices. Writing clarifies my process for me. I get a deeper understanding of what I'm trying to say. It's spiritual. It's my #1 way of connecting with God. The more I create, the more calm and connected I become.

It all happens when my mind wanders. I make a button look like a piece of candy: ●. I smack it right down in the middle of my painting. It's more than a button and some paint. It's textures: bumpy, smooth, rugged, hard, soft and gritty. It's colors: dark and light, cool and warm. Contrast, glowing, brightness. Screaming color. Child like. Always child like. I change one color and everything shifts. I'm always surprised when it's finished. "Done" is amazing. All this happens as my mind drifts and floats and wanders to places I don't even know it went.

Mix

Something to Try

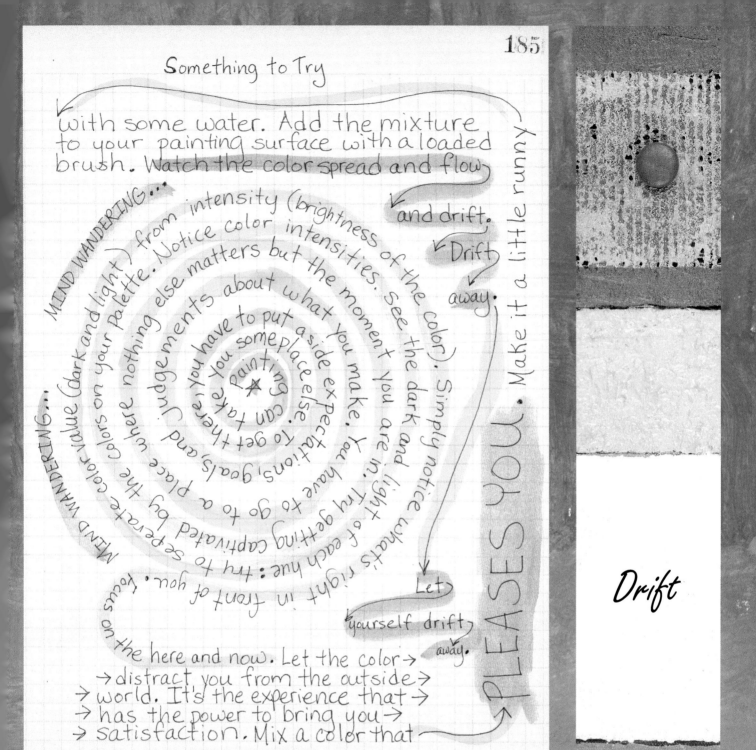

with some water. Add the mixture to your painting surface with a loaded brush. Watch the color spread and flow and drift. Drift away.

MIND WANDERING... from intensity (brightness of the color). Notice color intensities. See the dark and light of each hue: try to separate color from intensity (brightness of the color). Notice color intensities but the moment you are in. Try getting captivated by the color. Simply notice what's right in front of you. Focus on the here and now. Let the color → distract you from the outside → world. It's the experience that → has the power to bring you → satisfaction. Mix a color that PLEASES YOU. Make it a little runny.

MIND WANDERING... value (dark and light) colors on your palette where nothing else matters but the moment Judgements about what you make. You have to put aside expectations, goal(s) and someplace else you can take Painting. To get there, you have to go to a place where separate color by the

Let yourself drift away.

Drift

Something to Think About:

It's the experience that has the power to bring you satisfaction. Get captivated by the color. Study it and notice everything it does. Let yourself drift away into your own secret world.

Study

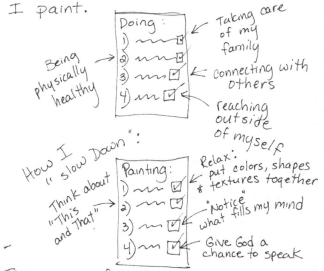

Slowing Down

I'm not really good at sitting still. In fact, I'm really terrible at it. Creating is an in-between: a space between my activity of my overactive mind and the state of being totally still. Totally still would be prayer: the thing I should be doing more often. I can't remember the last time I laid down in my room, put on some worship music, and just prayed.

On the other hand, I am constantly "Doing". I'm really good at "Doing" some pretty wonderful and important stuff. It's not all bad. Balance, for me, is the in-between. It's the place where I can slow down, reflect and still move and "Do". I can pray

in the "In-between". I can be quieter, slower and more peaceful in this place. The "In-between" is the place where I paint.

Doing:
1)
2) ← Being physically healthy
3)
4)

← Taking care of my family

← connecting with others

reaching outside of myself

How I "slow Down":

Painting:
1)
2) ← Think about "This and That"
3)
4)

Relax: put colors, shapes & textures together

"Notice" what fills my mind

Give God a chance to speak

This is my favorite way to slow down. It's how I was meant to make meaning and understand who I am meant to be. Paint, paint, paint...

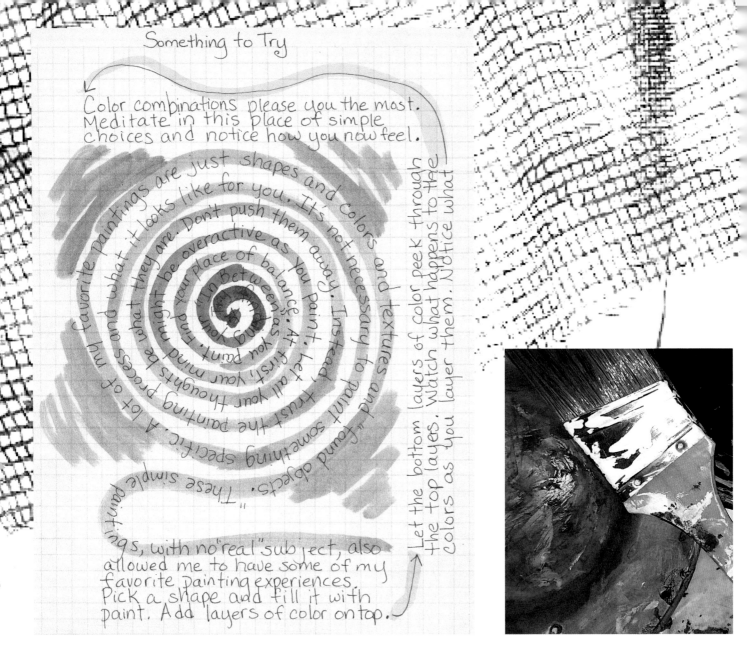

Something to Try

Color combinations please you the most. Meditate in this place of simple choices and notice how you now feel.

Favorite paintings are just shapes and colors and what it looks like for you. It's not necessary to paint something specific. Instead, trust the painting process. A lot of "found objects." These simple paintings, with no "real" subject, also allowed me to have some of my favorite painting experiences. Pick a shape and fill it with paint. Add layers of color on top.

Don't push them away as you paint. Let all your thoughts be overactive as you paint. At first, your mind might be in a place of balance. "In between" your mind and what they are.

Let the bottom layers of color peek through the top layers. Watch what happens to the colors as you layer them. Notice what

Something to Think About:

A simple object can become a tool for mindfulness painting. You can use the tool to focus on color without distractions. Are you anxious about making a mistake? Are you held back by the fear that you won't produce a pleasing product? A simple tool can help you relax and simplify the experience. The eraser on the end of a pencil is excellent for this. You just dip the end of the pencil into some paint and dab the color onto your canvas. This will make a dot of color. A jumbo pencil for preschoolers will have a slightly larger eraser. This will allow you to vary the size of your dot and allow you to place a smaller dot inside a larger one. An apple can be sliced in half and carved to create a stamp. Use it to make an even larger circle. Make a painting with just dots and circles of different pigments. Notice how the colors work together. Look for similar colors and notice how they work harmoniously. Consider how contrasting colors scream for attention and make themselves the focal point. Enjoy the way colors play together. Meditate on what you see. Note what you notice. Think about what it all means to you and how it makes you feel.

Note what you notice.

A simple activity that can be satisfying from beginning to end.

Painted Rocks by Ginger, Age 11

Something to Think About:

These rocks were painted by a child with limited experience creating mandala dot art. This is a great activity for anyone who wants to paint, regardless of their skill level. The process is very satisfying from beginning to end. You might want to purchase a "Mandala Dotting Kit" instead of using pencil eraser heads to give yourself a greater variety of dot sizes. Use acrylic paint and allow previous dots to dry before adding the next layer to reduce smearing. Sketch your pattern on your rock before you begin applying dots if that makes you feel more comfortable. Finally, mandala stencils are great for those who don't want to worry about creating their own sketch on their rock. All of these tips can help you stay focused on the pleasure of the painting experience.

Painted Rock by Daphne, Age 18

Watch what happens to the colors as you layer them.
Notice what color combinations please you the most.
Meditate in this place of simple choices.

Enjoy the way the colors play together.

Enjoy the way the colors play together. Meditate on what you see. Note what you notice. Think about what it all means to you and how it makes you feel.

Mandala Rocks Painted by a Family of "Beginners"

Pick an Object

Peacock feathers always point to my mom and my childhood. I keep making these collages, and peacock feathers often end up the focal point. I notice that this particular object brings back all kinds of memories: my childhood home, the 1960's & 1970's, my sister, what it felt like to be little, and the wild and funky wonderfullness of my mom. The peacock feather has an eye.

My grandmother, of Greek descent, always spoke of the "All Knowing Eye". The eye was always watching: especially if you were being bad. My "God's Eye" isn't like that because my God isn't like that. I know that He knows all — everything about me — but he's not judging me: I'm too good at judging me all on my own. My God always is softer on me than I am on myself. Please God, like what you see. Please God, help me see what you see. Please God, let me forgive me like you've already forgiven me. All of this meaning and thought is packed into this one simple object. I notice that it speaks so much more than anyone will see when they look at what I create. GOD KNOWS.

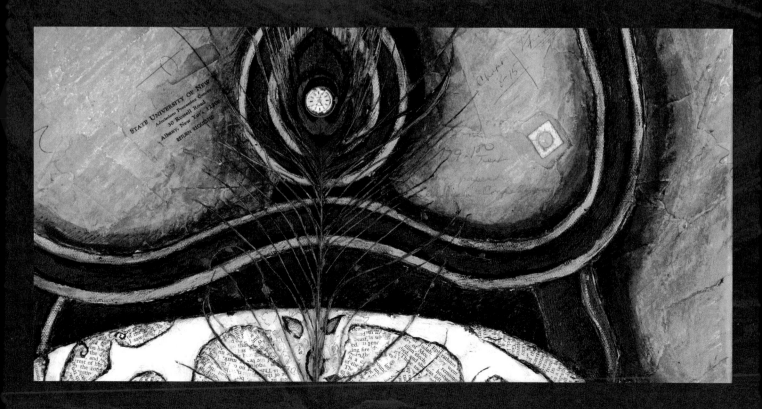

Something to Try

exhilaration. Notice how you feel in these moments. Embrace it and let it be what it is......

Think about how you can incorporate this object into your design.

Will you paint over it (put a layer of gesso over it first if you decide on this)? Will you leave it intact? Then, paint around it! Figure out how to get it all to come together in a way that satisfies you. Meditating on these types of creative decisions can bring you into a private world of deep personal meaning and symbolism. In these moments you can feel intense calm or great

Pick an embellishment or something to add to your painting. What will it be for you. For me, it's often a peacock feather. Glue it down somewhere on the surface of your creation. It could be a flower, a pendant, a cross, a button or a bead. Go on a hunt for something that means something to you.

Paint for you.

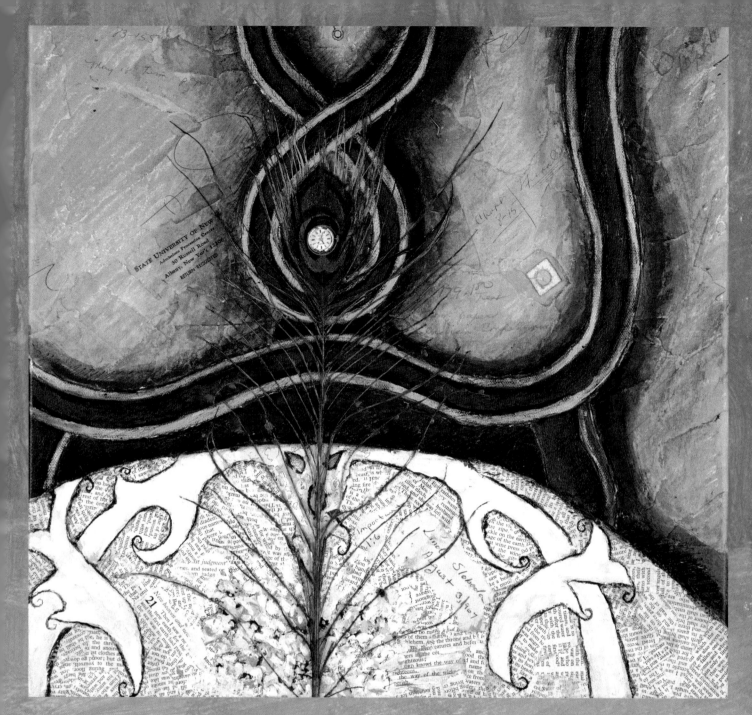

Watch Findings, 2016

Something to Think About:

Objects can be added to your paintings. They can hold special meaning for you, and sometimes it is just easier to add the object to your artwork than it is to try and recreate an image or symbol for it. There is absolutely no reason why you can't plop something right down in the middle of your canvas. You can paint over it or just leave it intact. It's totally up to you. I enjoy feeling and exploring an object before I find a spot for it inside my work. I notice the textures and colors. I might even smell it if it has an odor. Sometimes, this process reminds me of things I have forgotten: things associated with the object that did not immediately come to mind. It's a little extra meditation time that I weave into the painting process. I have boxes full of objects. Whenever I come across something meaningful, I add it to my collection and wait for the perfect moment to use it. Collecting the objects is part of the fun. I also find this process centering and calming. The collecting helps me notice the things that fill my mind. Most of all, it makes my painting time richer. Focusing on the object keeps me mindful of the "Here and Now." I leave all my worries and concerns behind. All I see and do is paint.

Gratitude

My mom's things are aging right along with her. I inherited this lovely purse that Mom once wore to gala events. She had a way of looking smashing with her unique, eclectic style and charisma. I always thought my mom was more beautiful than anyone else's mom. You might think I was biased, but it was true. Lovely Purse has seen better days. It is irreparable. The lining is torn and shredded. The beads are falling off. I considered restoration, but its condition is too far gone to turn back the clock. It's an analogy for what has happened to my mom over time. Time doesn't

If it can't be what it once was, it might as well be seen: right smack in the middle of my painting. rob me of my gratitude, though.

I pour out my gratitude as I paint about Smashing, Beautiful Mom. I see that Lovely Purse must be the focal point. I spend great amounts of time thinking about my gratitude for Lovely Purse and how it's just like my mom.

glitzy! so glitzy, she lit up the room!

snazzy: the queen of snazz!

unique

Inside, it's frayed and worn. Outside, too. I am grateful for what is and what was.

lovely;

Mom wasn't perfect, but her heart was in the right place.

exquisite

No one saw her "exquisite" more than Dad and I am so grateful for that, too.

Gratitude, gratitude, gratitude, gratitude, gratitude, gratitude, gratitude.

I paint and I keep returning to gratitude. Gratitude, gratitude, gratitude......

Something to Try

the painting takes you. It's about what you learn and what you feel in the process. It's about the freedom it brings. It can all begin with "gratitude!"

With each stroke of your brush think "gratitude."

What will you pick for a theme. I picked "gratitude." Try Painting on "gratitude." Use your theme as a

What theme will you consider as you paint today?

the world around you. A point of focus can slow your mind down and allow you to relax. It can help you notice things that allow for a richer experience of life. It's not about your painting. It's about where

point of focus. Or, maybe it just ends up being a spring board to another loosely related place? That's OK too. You can be mindful of things like "gratitude" when you paint. This can bring you deeper insight into yourself and how you interact with

Something to Think About:

As you paint, choose a focus word such as gratitude, forgiveness, compassion or kindness. As your mind wanders, gently return to your focus word. As you move and mix your paint, create textures and layer colors. Let your mind contemplate and ponder. Meditating on a simple word as you paint can give you new insight and a deeper understanding of yourself and others. Consider that this process is not actually about your painting. It's about where your painting takes you.

Gratitude, forgiveness, compassion?????

Anxiety

Painting helps me quiet my thoughts. I am fully aware of everything I'm thinking— totally conscious, but the thoughts I think (good and bad) are humming instead of screaming. My mind often drifts to places where bad things happened, but as I paint things melt and resolve. I reach into my Random Stuff Jar and pull out the Slop Sink Plug that plugged the laundry room sink: the place I was bathed when I was really small.

* My anxiety quiets and I am quiet inside I paint in peace.

I notice a small surge of anxiety, grab the glue, and pop the plug right in the center of a square in a painting. I'm fully aware that this is an anxiety origin: a place in my life where fear originated. My mom would pull that plug and I would be filled with fear. I was convinced I would get sucked down the unplugged hole. Today, I quietly see the plug with a new quiet inside. I see it for what it was: a moment of childish misunderstanding. I also see it for what it is: the truth that the things I fear aren't such a great cause for fear. *

Random stuff Jar

at the end of my bath ↑plug

vortex ↓ hole

Something to Try

have a place in your painting might be "something to try."

thin brush

buttons

Palette Knife

...reach out for help, too. Stuff will come up as you paint, that's something to notice. You might need to act and reach out for help, too. If you notice anxiety, fear, anger or frustration when you paint, that's something to notice. "Stuffing your stuff" won't likely make the feelings go away. In fact, painting can make you understand both the positive and negative in a new way. If you notice feelings, letting them...

All kinds of feelings can have a place on a canvas!

fat brush

fanbrush

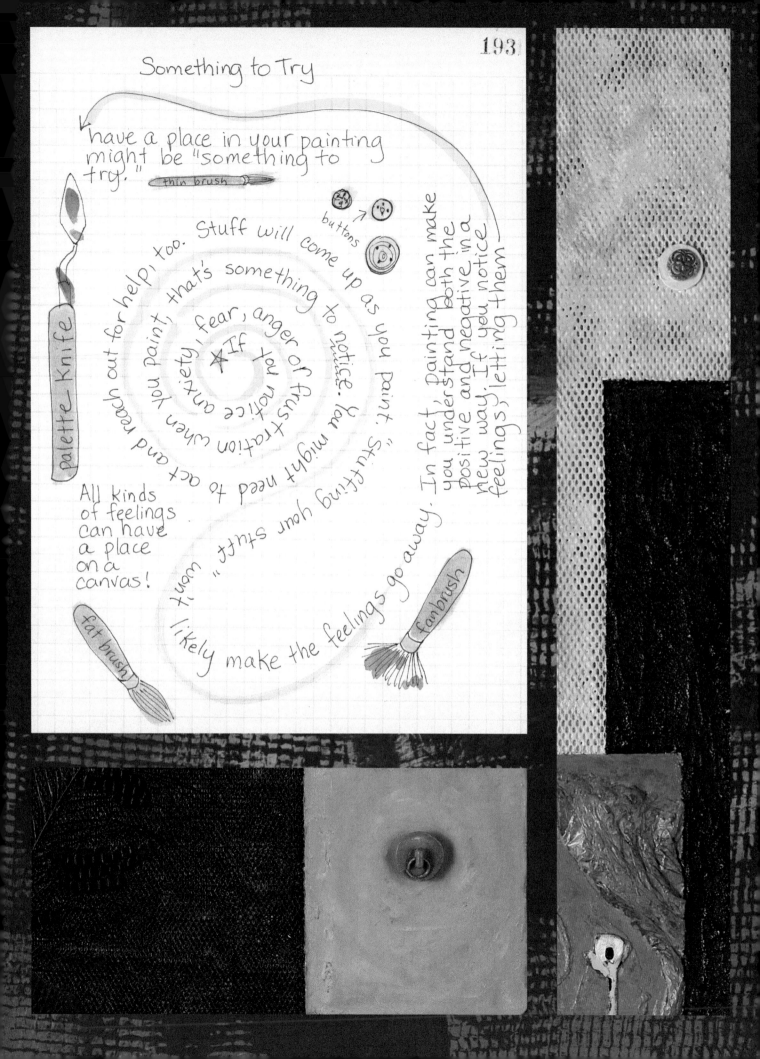

Playing with Color

I see that color has no rules. One person loves purple and hates orange and that's true for them. Another person loves orange and hates purple and that's their truth. We get to decide.

↑
Is green against pink ugly? Or, is it beautiful???

THERE IS NO "TRUTH", ONLY

"YOUR TRUTH"....

and

there is ENORMOUS

freedom to be found here.

My mind drifts and my palette shifts. Sometimes I don't remember where my mind went: it has been floating for hours. I experience an empty mind that's free to not think. It makes choices I am unaware of until I make a mark on my canvas. Call it mindfulness. Call it mindlessness. Either way, this is a place to find freedom.

I haven't worried for hours. I just think about the colors.

Play! ↓

↙ Be free!